VELO CITY

ARCHITECTURE FOR BIKES

GAVIN BLYTH

PRESTEL
Munich · London · New York

CONTENTS

CYCLING
AND THE CITY

The bicycle is beginning to have a profound impact on the development of our towns and cities, informing and driving new design typologies that range from novel forms of parking to bike-specific bridges and tunnels.

Burgeoning subcultures based around cycling's many different disciplines are carving out spaces - both official and unofficial - in the world's major cities. New shops and clubs are springing up to support them, presenting architects and designers with fresh opportunities and challenges.

Above all, cycling in cities provides us with an instant snapshot of their architecture and industry, culture and social mores. The only way to get such a picture is by bike; by car you become disconnected from your surroundings, while on foot you lose the momentum that highlights the step changes in the fabric of the city.

CYCLE
CONSUMPTION

CYCLE
CONSUMPTION

The ever-increasing popularity of cycling is being driven and supported by a growing number of manufacturers and stores who cater to cyclists' every need. Architects are now designing shops to display these products that owe more to fashion boutiques or art galleries than the grimy, cluttered bike stores of yesterday.

Whether you're an urban hipster or serious roadie, vintage enthusiast or commuter, the options now open to you are limited only by your imagination. The idea that both your bike and the clothes in which you ride it can be customised to reflect your own style and personality is particularly prevalent in the fixed-gear scene.

Adherents of the fixed-gear bike can be found cycling slowly and deliberately - both as a way to see and be seen, and as a consequence of having no brakes - around cities such as London or San Francisco. Sometimes disparagingly referred to as 'fakengers', these poseurs borrow their style and their bikes from the world of cycle couriers, who have traditionally used them because of their strength and simplicity.

Grayscaled's designs for the Mission Bicycle Store in San Francisco draw heavily on the customisation aspect of the fixed-gear scene as well as the inherent simplicity of the bikes themselves. This apparent contradiction has created a store that is both simple in its execution yet complex in its interactions. As the store is based in a former mortuary, the architects created a series of cabinets akin to the slabs on which post-mortems are carried out. Here, bicycle components are laid out like a mortician's tools, enabling the customer to specify everything from a sprocket to a headset, in any colour they choose so long as it's not black. The open assembly work area allows customers to engage with the bike mechanics, watch their bicycle being built, and learn about its upkeep.

At the other end of the spectrum, high-end cycle-clothing manufacturer Rapha treats its flagship stores as clubs where like-minded roadies can meet for coffee, attend screenings or of course simply buy some of Rapha's beautifully designed cycling wear.

Their London store, designed by Brinkworth in 2012, reflects Rapha's attention to detail and respect for the sport of cycling. In the café, the counter is topped by zinc in a nod to European café culture, and the company's signature pink, grey and white palette is used throughout. A Citroën H Van, the vehicle traditionally used in the fifties and sixties as a broom wagon for the Tour de France, lurks in a corner, while the painted grey concrete floors, combined with breezeblock walls and open ceilings, add to the workshop aesthetic.

For those less interested in speed or getting their hands dirty, Tokyobike, established in Japan in 2002, offers a more relaxed alternative. The bikes are designed around the concept of 'Tokyo Slow', in which the journey is just as important as the destination. These unashamedly urban bikes place the emphasis firmly on comfort and style rather than out-and-out speed. For their flagship store in London's fashionable Shoreditch, designers Glass Hill created a shop which at first glance looks more like an art gallery than a bike store. Like sculptures, the bicycles are displayed on plinths against plain white walls that allow the bright colours of the bikes to stand out. Materials and fittings, which are kept to a minimum, consist of white melamine board together with oiled Douglas-fir floorboards.

For its Berlin branch, Tokyobike commissioned local architects StudioCE. Uniquely, StudioCE also have their studio in the shop, which architect Holger Schwarz describes as the ideal partnership: "The combination of bike shop and architectural practice has generated interesting partnerships throughout the city and beyond. Clients have fallen in love with the bikes and turned into customers, while bike customers have given us the opportunity to build their homes. The symbiosis is working very well and both sides of the business profit from their surroundings."

TOKYOBIKE STORE
LONDON, UK 2012
GLASS HILL

For Tokyobike the journey
is just as important as
the destination. The concept
of 'Tokyo Slow' is the key
driver in the design of these
unashamedly urban bikes -
available with or without
gears - that emphasise
comfort and style rather
than speed. Tokyobike's
London flagship store is
housed in a former gallery
in the fashionable and fixed-
gear savvy Shoreditch area.

Materials and fittings are kept to a minimum: white melamine board together with oiled Douglas-fir floorboards and white walls provide the perfect backdrop for Tokyobike's colourful yet pared-down designs.

Like sculptures in an art gallery, the bicycles are displayed on plinths, the stark white walls both reinforcing this reference and allowing the bright colours of the bikes to stand out.

TOKYOBIKE STORE
BERLIN, GERMANY 2012
STUDIOCE

The Tokyobike store in Berlin's Kreuzberg district is unique in that it shares its space with the architects who designed it. The store cleverly integrates disparate functions, providing visual links between showroom and studio, meeting room and workshop.

The centrepiece for the store is an integral display wall made from dark plywood on which the bikes are hung much like pictures in an art gallery. The architecture studio is adjacent to the display wall and sits on a raised platform made from the same material.

The studio/shop is a synthesis of StudioCE's architectural ideas and the minimal design ethos of Tokyobike's bicycle. The store provides a showcase for both and has turned architectural clients into customers for bikes and Tokyobike customers into clients for StudioCE's work.

SPREAD BICYCLE CONCEPT STORE
HONG KONG, CHINA 2011
EUREKA

In keeping with GUM's green
credentials, the façade
was clad with hand-creased
recycled laminated paper.

GUM (Green Urban Mobility),
a Hong Kong-based cycling
advocacy group, opened
their first shop in the
city in 2011. Designed
to function as much as
a gallery and event space
as a shop, Spread holds
regular bike-related
screenings, launches
and events.

Inspired by a pin-art toy, the 'Play and Display' wall is made up of 5,412 recycled paper tubes on which products can be nestled, leant, cradled or hung.

GREGG'S CYCLES
BELLEVUE, WASHINGTON DC, USA 2007
WEINSTEIN A|U

Bicycles are suspended across
the length and breadth of
the huge display window,
simultaneously animating
the façade and acting as
a large-scale advertisement
for the shop's products.

Clearly expressed throughout, the building's steel frame, together with open steel stairs and exposed services, lends the space an industrial, engineered aesthetic that mirrors the structural economy of the bicycle.

The shop is a simple steel box elevated above ground level and cantilevered out over the street; any architectural bravado has been kept to a minimum leaving the bicycles to do the talking.

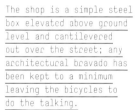

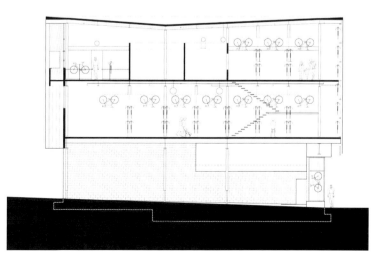

CYCLIST.GR
ATHENS, GREECE 2011
REACT ARCHITECTS

The materials used in the interior extend beyond the building's threshold, blurring the distinction between outside and inside space. A 150m² mezzanine level is given over to clothing and accessories.

The 400m² ground floor acts as the main display space for bicycles. Organised into separate sections for city, mountain, road and children's bicycles, the floor surface used in each reflects the different cycling disciplines: artificial grass for mountain and children's bikes and aggregate for road and city.

Oriented strand board is used throughout the store, providing the main material for shelving, walls and floors while acting as a directional walkway for customers and unifying the whole structure.

DOMAIN BICYCLE WORKSHOP
SAN FRANCISCO, USA 2011
GRAYSCALED DESIGN

San Francisco has some of
the highest per capita bike
use in the USA; the map
stencilled onto the wall
shows the Oakland/Alameda
area in which the project is
located, the dots represent
different Bay Area Rapid
Transit (BART) stations.

All members of the Grayscaled team are enthusiastic riders of fixed-gear bikes, the simplicity of which informed their approach to the Domain Bicycle Workshop. A pared down palette of plywood shelving and fittings provides a robust and economical solution.

A full set of tools is made available in the workshop so that residents can service and repair their bicycles. Bikes are available to hire and are supplied by the Mission Bicycle Store - also designed by the practice.

MISSION BICYCLE STORE
SAN FRANCISCO, USA 2009
GRAYSCALED DESIGN

In reference to the shop's former life as a mortuary, Grayscaled designed a number of backlit cabinets to display the various components that go into making a Mission Bicycle, much like a mortician's tools on the autopsy table.

The architects conceived of the shop as a 'curiosity boutique', arranging the individual components to promote interaction with the customer and emphasise the almost limitless customisation available to them with a Mission Bicycle. By suspending completed bicycles from the ceiling, the architects wanted to convey the dynamism and pleasure of riding a bicycle through space.

Mission Bicycle's holistic
approach to bike purchasing
is reinforced further
through the open assembly
work area which allows
customers to engage with
the bike mechanics, watch
their bicycle being built,
and learn about its upkeep.

RAPHA CYCLE CLUB
LONDON, UK 2012
BRINKWORTH

Founded in 2004, Rapha manufactures some of the world's finest cycling apparel. With an emphasis on road racing, the company has managed to pull off that rare balancing act of creating clothing that both performs to the highest levels and also looks stylish.

Rapha's signature pink, grey and white palette is used throughout the club, which is also home to their Citroën H Van, the vehicle traditionally used in the fifties and sixties as a broom wagon for the Tour de France.

Rapha's flagship store in London's Soho acts a meeting place for like-minded cyclists, providing a place to watch racing, to eat, and of course to purchase Rapha products.

Solid-concrete floors painted grey, combined with breezeblock walls and open ceilings with exposed conduit and trunking, lend the space a workshop feel that is entirely in keeping with the sport.

The materials used throughout the club reflect Rapha's attention to detail and respect for the sport of cycling. In the café, the counter is topped by zinc in a nod to European café culture, while visitors sit down at tables etched with some of Europe's greatest climbs.

Cycling memorabilia shares floor and wall space with Rapha products. A flexible racking system was developed so that shelving could be moved out of the way to open up the space for larger events.

BIKE FIXTATION – PUBLIC WORK STANDS
VARIOUS LOCATIONS USA 2011
ALEX ANDERSON AND CHAD DEBAKER

As well as having tools, work stands are fitted with a QR code that provides links to repair instructions, so that even novices are able to continue their journey.

Bike Fixtation is a self-service bike repair station designed and developed by Minneapolis cycling enthusiasts Alex Anderson and Chad DeBaker. First installed in Minneapolis' Uptown Transit Station in 2011, the modular system is now being rolled out across the United States.

Each Fixtation comprises
a vending machine containing
essentials such as inner tubes,
patches and lights, together
with an air compressor.
This is accompanied by a
work stand to which various
tools are attached, ensuring
most repairs can be carried
out in situ.

ON THE
RIGHT TRACK

ON THE
RIGHT TRACK

Since the completion of its first cycle track in 1885, the Netherlands has gone on to lead the world in cycling-related infrastructure. It now boasts the highest per capita rate of cycle use in the world, together with the greatest number of cycle lanes. It was unique in developing cycle tracks in tandem with its roads. The idea that cyclists should have their own distinct space has created an infrastructure which is peculiar to the Netherlands; for while piecemeal development has occurred elsewhere, no other country, apart from Denmark, has achieved such a systematic and comprehensive cycling infrastructure.

Whereas in the Netherlands there is a uniformity to the design of cycle tracks, sharing common road markings and signage, this is absent in the United Kingdom. There are indications that things are beginning to change, however. The introduction of the Barclays Cycle Hire scheme in London in 2010 not only gave people the opportunity to hire a bicycle but also introduced new cycle superhighways and a bespoke signage system to the capital.

However, what is most noticeable about the scheme is its livery: the entire thing, from bikes to bollards, is painted in Barclays' corporate shade of blue. Even Edward Johnson's iconic red and navy-blue roundel, originally commissioned for the London Underground and since adopted by London Transport, has been redone in the corporate colours of Barclays Bank. One is never in any doubt that the scheme was part funded by the bank. Even the new superhighways have been painted blue, which, coincidentally, is the colour of the UK Conservative Party, of which London Mayor and instigator of the scheme, Boris Johnson, is a representative.

Copenhagen's 359 kilometres of cycle tracks, signage and infrastructure are unencumbered by such gratuitous advertising. The city is criss-crossed by a comprehensive network of cycle tracks that are entirely state funded. The self-styled 'city of cyclists' has more bicycles than people, who on average ride a total of 1.2 million kilometres per day.

In an attempt to get more people cycling into the centre of the city from the suburbs, the mayor is introducing a series of Green Cycle Routes. A total of 22 routes covering 110 kilometres are planned by 2026. These are separated from the rest of the infrastructure and have minimal contact with traffic. Because of their width, these act as motorways for cyclists, providing those residents who live out of the city centre with a viable alternative to public transport or motorcars for longer journeys.

The initiative's centrepiece is the Ågade Bridge, which links Copenhagen's Nørrebro quarter with the Frederiksberg Municipality. Designed by local firm Dissing + Weitling and completed in 2008, the bridge has become an instantly recognisable landmark for the city and a valuable resource for pedestrians and cyclists alike, who until now had to try and negotiate four lanes of traffic on one of Copenhagen's busiest streets.

A further innovation designed to secure Copenhagen's reputation as the city of cyclists has taken place on a domestic rather than urban scale. BIG architects' 8 House allows cyclists to ride from their front door, which can be up to ten floors high, all the way down to ground level without ever getting out of the saddle.

The building rises and falls along its perimeter, reaching ten storeys at its north-eastern tip and dropping to ground level at its south-western corner. This arrangement not only optimises the differing light and shade requirements for office and residential accommodation, but also enables the continuous cycle path. Running alongside terraced gardens and balconies, this provides the cyclist with an interactive neighbourhood experience akin to that found in an Italian hill town or village. By placing the bike at the heart of the development rather than hiding it away in a basement bike park, BIG are able to facilitate the kind of daily interactions and sense of community which are often absent in more traditional residential blocks.

ARGANZUELA FOOTBRIDGE
MADRID, SPAIN 2011
DOMINIQUE PERRAULT ARCHITECTURE

As in the wider park,
cyclists share the bridge
with pedestrians.

The Arganzuela Footbridge
is the longest in a series
of bridges planned for
Madrid's Manzanares Park, a
new recreation area on both
sides of the Manzanares river
made possible after one of
the city's major highways was
buried underground.

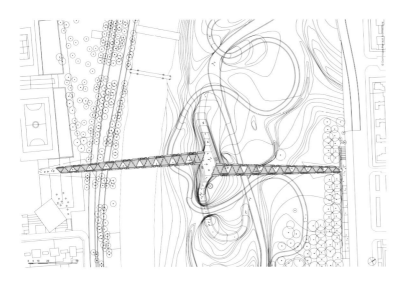

Conical in structure, the bridge, which is made up of two sections that meet at the highest point, provides both an entrance to the park and spectacular views of the historic Toledo Bridge beyond.

A slatted wooden deck ensures that daylight filters through to the park below.

The spiralling steel structure creates a metallic ribbon effect across the park. Part open, part enclosed by a fine mesh, the bridge changes throughout the day according to the position of the sun, while at night it becomes lit up like a lantern.

BARCLAYS CYCLE HIRE
LONDON, UK 2010
TRANSPORT FOR LONDON

The Barclays Cycle Hire scheme uses an off-the-shelf system first developed for Montreal's BIXI Public Bike Scheme. Designed by Michel Dallaire Design Industriel Inc, the bikes and docking system can now be found in cities across the world. A system of cycle super-highways was introduced at the same time to provide safer, faster routes from outer London to the city.

Londoners have embraced the scheme, dubbing the bicycles 'Boris Bikes' after Boris Johnson, the London Mayor who introduced the scheme in 2010. There are now 8,000 bikes located across 570 docking stations.

The entire scheme from
bicycles to cycle
superhighways is branded
in Barclays' corporate
shade of blue.

HOVENRING BRIDGE
EINDHOVEN, THE NETHERLANDS 2012
IPV DELFT

The architects' desire to create as much transparency and openness as possible has resulted in an incredibly economical structure. Twenty-four tensioned cables link the counterweighted inner ring to a 70-metre central mast to ensure torsional stability, while a series of M-shaped steel supports at each of the four entrances carry the deck.

As befits Eindhoven's status as the Netherland's City of Light, the Hovenring benefits from a spectacular lighting scheme: the mast is washed with purple light and the railings incorporate LEDs. The system of tubular lighting sandwiched between the inner and outer deck reinforces the lightweight, transparent nature of the structure.

This is cycling infrastructure on a grandiose scale. Owing more to the language of a motorway intersection than to a suburban bike path, this floating disc 72 metres in diameter allows cyclists to negotiate one of the Netherland's busiest roads with ease.

MELKWEGBRIDGE
PURMEREND, THE NETHERLANDS 2012
NEXT ARCHITECTS

The Melkwegbridge's vertiginous 12-metre high arch gives pedestrians spectacular views of the city and forms a new focal point for the southern end of the Melkweg, the road which bisects the historic heart of the city.

The Melkwegbridge crosses
the Noordhollandsch Kanaal,
connecting the historic
centre of Purmerend with
the emerging district of
Weidevenne in the southwest.

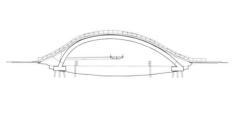

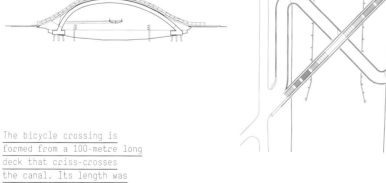

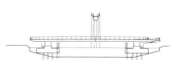

The bicycle crossing is
formed from a 100-metre long
deck that criss-crosses
the canal. Its length was
dictated by the difference
in height between the two
banks and the subsequent
local authority minimum-slope
requirements for bicycles and
wheelchairs.

The Melkwegbridge's novel arrangement successfully segregates cyclists from pedestrians while still allowing easy passage for boats. To allow boats to pass, the cycling deck splits in two, pivoting around two piers on either side of the canal, while the arch's 12-metre height ensures that pedestrian access remains uninterrupted.

ÅGADE BRIDGE
COPENHAGEN, DENMARK 2008
DISSING+WEITLING

In an attempt to get more
people cycling into the
centre of the city from
Copenhagen's suburbs, the
mayor is introducing a series
of Green Cycle Routes, of
which the Ågade Bridge is
the centrepiece.

Curved in both plan and
section, the bridge is
supported by an elegant
steel arch.

The bridge has become an instantly recognisable landmark for the city and a valuable resource for pedestrians and cyclists alike, who until now had to negotiate several lanes of traffic on one of Copenhagen's busiest streets.

VÉLIB' BICYCLE HIRE SCHEME
PARIS, FRANCE 2007
JCDECAUX

The scheme is financed and run by advertising company JCDecaux, who in return receive exclusive control of more than 1,500 of the city's advertising billboards.

Vélib' is a conflation of velo, meaning bicycle, and liberté, meaning freedom. The cycle-share scheme was launched in 2007 and has over 20,000 bikes distributed across 1,800 stations. Designed for comfort and reliability, the bikes contain no exposed cables and benefit from a covered chain and step-through frame.

Both the bikes and street furniture were designed exclusively for the Vélib' scheme by JCDecaux's in-house team led by Patrick Jouin. The subdued grey colour scheme was chosen to blend in with the existing urban environment.

8 HOUSE
COPENHAGEN, DENMARK 2010
BIG ARCHITECTS

The 8 House allows cyclists to ride from their front door, which can be up to ten floors high, all the way down to ground level without ever getting out of the saddle.

As the name implies, the
8 House is figure-of-eight
shaped in plan. Office and
retail accommodation occupy
the lower floors, with
residential accommodation
occupying the space above.
This creates two enclosed
courtyard parks, separated
by a vertical spine that
contains communal facilities.

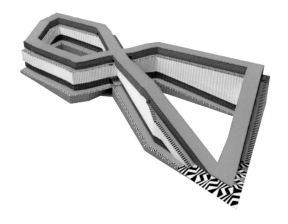

By placing the bike at the
heart of the development
rather than hiding it away
in a basement bike park, BIG
are able to facilitate the
kind of daily interactions
and sense of community
which are often absent in
more controlled residential
blocks.

The building rises and falls
along it perimeter, reaching
ten storeys at its north-
eastern tip and dropping
to ground level at its south-
western corner. This arrangement
not only optimises the differing
light and shade requirements
for office and residential
accommodation, but also
facilitates the continuous
cycle path.

The cycle path runs alongside
terraced gardens and
balconies, providing the
cyclist with an interactive
neighbourhood experience akin
to that found in an Italian
hill town or village.

BRYGGE BRIDGE
COPENHAGEN, DENMARK 2006
DISSING+WEITLING

Connecting Havneholmen and
Islandsbrygg, the bridge
forms a narrow, gently arced
spine that swings open across
one of its spans to allow
tall ships to pass through.

Completed in 2006, the
Brygge Bridge was the first
to have been built across
Copenhagen Harbour for 50
years. Perhaps unsurprisingly
for the self-styled city of
cyclists, the bridge is for
the exclusive use of cyclists
and pedestrians.

The design adopts the same
pared-down language as its
Ågade neighbour, except in
this case it is supported by
a series of slender piers
rather than an arch.

A central reservation
segregates pedestrians from
cyclists, though, as in the
rest of the city, the two
groups appear to coexist
quite happily.

BICYCLE SHARING SCHEME
VILAMOURA, PORTUGAL 2012
AND-RÉ

As well as designing the bikes, multidisciplinary design practice AND-RÉ was responsible for the signage, maps and electronic cards used to release the bikes. There are currently 37 pick-up and drop-off points, together with 200 bicycles.

Residents of the luxury resort in Portugal's Algarve have enthusiastically embraced the bicycle-sharing scheme, which is ideally suited to the area's mild climate and flat terrain.

Despite having the robustness and functionality needed for any public bike, Vilamoura bicycles have a luxury, bespoke feel. The designers pared back the bicycle to its essential elements, referencing both vintage and fixed-gear bicycles.

The scheme is open to residents of the resort, who for a monthly or yearly subscription gain unlimited access to the bikes for periods of up to 45 minutes at a time.

BIKEWAY BELÉM
LISBON, PORTUGAL 2012
P-06 ATELIER AND
GLOBAL LANDSCAPE ARCHITECTS

Extracts from Portuguese poet
Alberto Caeiro's poem about
the river Tagus appear at
strategic points along
the route.

The Bikeway Belém runs for 7 km along the banks of the river Tagus in Lisbon. The bold, white wayfinding system, which is painted directly onto the path, provides cyclists with directions, distance travelled, and points of interest.

Combining bold graphic design
with poetry and humour, the
Bikeway Belém is a stunning
example of how the often
overlooked art of wayfinding
and signage can be turned
into something extraordinary
and uplifting.

DUBAI CYCLE TRACK
UNITED ARAB EMIRATES 2012
DUBAI ROADS & TRANSPORT AUTHORITY

As well as enduring
temperatures of up to 45
degrees, cyclists can
encounter a variety of
wildlife, including oryx
and camels.

Completed in 2012, the Dubai
Cycle Track is a 68-km
cycle superhighway in the
middle of the desert.
It was built at the request
of Dubai's ruler Sheikh
Mohammed bin Rashid, who
after encountering ever
increasing numbers of
cyclists en route to his
stables, thought a dedicated
cycle path would be safer.
The course consists of a
50-km loop with an additional
18 km of track leading up
to it enabling cyclists to
enjoy safe, rapid cycling
on wide, purpose-built
asphalt tracks.

PEACE BRIDGE
CALGARY, CANADA 2012
SANTIAGO CALATRAVA

The 126-metre long single-span bridge is formed from an open double helix structure which, while rigorously mathematical in its planning, appears effortlessly organic in its execution. Fritted-glass 'leaves' bent to shape fill the uppermost apertures to protect against the elements.

The bridge connects the residential Sunnyside area on the north bank of the Bow River with the downtown community of Eau Claire to the south. The 2.5-metre wide bicycle lane occupies the centre of the bridge and is flanked on either side by 1.85-metre wide pedestrian paths.

The Peace Bridge's red livery
marks a departure from
Calatrava's usual monochrome
palette and provides a
striking year-round contrast
to its surroundings, which
vary from lush green to
snow white depending on
the season.

MACHINES FOR
PARKING BICYCLES IN

MACHINES FOR
PARKING BICYCLES IN

Renowned architectural historian Nikolaus Pevsner wrote in 1943 that "a bicycle shed is a building; Lincoln cathedral is a piece of architecture". However, if he were still around today - he died in 1983 after completing 46 county-by-county guides to England's architecture, his seminal 'The Buildings of England' - would he still use the bike shed as his exemplar? Given the flurry of creative activity in this sphere over the past ten years, it seems unlikely. Back in 1943, the bike shed was exactly that - a shed, a consciously un-designed afterthought consisting of little more than a corrugated-iron canopy.

Today, that could not be further from the truth. The Netherlands alone could be credited with having elevated the bicycle shed to architectural status, so what should it be called now? 'Cycle station' or 'bike park', perhaps - after all, both car parks and train stations made it into Pevsner's lexicon of architecture. For example, in Groningen architectural and planning firm KCAP Architects&Planners have managed to address the need for bicycle parking at the city's station while simultaneously carving out a new pedestrianised square. The Stadsbalkon, or 'city balcony', consists of a winged deck which gently slopes away to create a plaza, the top of which is reserved for pedestrians. Below this lies parking for up to 4,000 bikes and a subterranean route that enables cyclists to pass unhindered beneath the plaza.

There are over 4,000 bike-parking facilities in Copenhagen, with space for almost 50,000 bikes. To date, the city has favoured an on-street approach to bicycle storage rather than the subterranean or multi-storey solutions used in the Netherlands. This approach has largely been dictated by a desire to take more cars off the roads. By transforming on-street car-parking spaces into bicycle parking, motorists are gradually being forced out of the city centre. These range from simple parking zones which do not contain any racks and are marked out by white lines painted on the road, much like car-parking bays, to more elaborate racking systems which are integrated with existing street furniture.

It's significant that the winning entry in a competition to redevelop the city's Nørreport rail station - the busiest in Denmark - has been designed around the bicycle. Designed by local firms COBE and Gottlieb

Paludan Architects, the station has been conceived as a large outdoor plaza punctuated by a series of circular pavilions. These transparent enclosures, which are topped by large, irregularly shaped overhanging roofs, house the station's various functions. Interspersed among the pavilions are a number of 'bike beds'. These storage facilities place the bike at the centre of the scheme in a series of beds that are recessed 40 cm into the plaza.

> A recent initiative in the city graphically illustrates the amount of space cars take up relative to bicycles. Recognising the increasing popularity of cargo bikes in Copenhagen - 6 per cent of households now own one - the city council commissioned design firm Goodmorning Technology to come up with a solution for storing the bikes overnight and in bad weather. The result, CarGo, is a car-shaped fibreglass shell capable of housing four cargo bikes. This witty addition to Copenhagen's streets encapsulates the city's attitude to creating a sustainable car-free environment.

Both Amsterdam and Copenhagen have successfully integrated the bicycle into modern urban life. In these cities the bicycle is the most convenient way to get around thanks to the innovative and extensive provision of infrastructure developed to support it. However, even in those cities with a less enlightened or hostile attitude to cycling, some interesting bicycle sheds are beginning to emerge.

> The first bicycle transit centre to be completed on the east coast of America is a highly visible addition to Washington DC's historic Union Station. Designed to promote bicycle use in the city, its form echoes the shape of a bicycle helmet, while its structural logic is informed by the bicycle wheel. A series of arched steel tubes - held in compression at either end by a pair of concrete wedges - span the structure much like the rim of a wheel. Inside, the centre has parking for 150 bicycles, as well as changing facilities, lockers and a workshop.

By placing such an uncompromisingly modern building next to the Beaux-Arts splendour of Union Station, its designers, KGP Design Studio, are asking us to consider the bicycle on equal terms with the train as an alternative mode of transport for the twenty-first century, a sentiment shared by many of the other designers featured in this book.

CARGO, OUTLINE AND CUSTOM BIKE STAND
VARIOUS LOCATIONS 2009
GOODMORNING TECHNOLOGY

The CarGo is a car-shaped
fibreglass shell capable of
protecting up to four cargo
bikes from the extremes of
Copenhagen's weather. The
front and rear of the 'car'
pivot open to allow access.

The Outline, Goodmorning
Technology's latest solution
for cargo-bike parking,
offers temporary secure
parking for four bikes.
Like the CarGo, the Outline
takes the form of a car,
though in this case it's a
simple frame of galvanised
steel. The CarGo comes
complete with solar-powered
headlights and tail lights
that come on automatically
at night; the Outline can be
specified with luminous paint.

Goodmorning Technology's
Custom Bike Stand can be
manufactured to spell out
any name or product and
can be either permanently
fixed outdoors or used as
a temporary solution.

Frederiksberg council,
a Copenhagen municipality,
ordered several FRB-branded
Custom Bike Stands to
communicate their green,
bike-friendly strategy
and vision.

STADSBALKON
GRONINGEN, THE NETHERLANDS 2007
KCAP ARCHITECTS & PLANNERS

There is parking for up to 4,000 bikes together with a subterranean route that enables cyclists to pass beneath the plaza.

The Stadsbalkon or city balcony has been designed so as not to hinder views of the recently restored train station. It consists of a winged deck that gently slopes away to create a plaza, the top of which is reserved for pedestrians. Large circular holes have been punched through the balcony in a number of places to enable natural light to illuminate the bike park below.

BICYCLE WAREHOUSE
ZAANDAM, THE NETHERLANDS 2011
NUNC ARCHITECTEN

Amsterdam's Fietsenpakhuis,
which has free-of-charge
daily parking facilities
for 700 bikes, was designed
to help take congestion and
clutter from Zaandam's main
shopping avenue.

Located in Amsterdam's
historic industrial area of
Zaandam, the Fietsenpakhuis
(bicycle warehouse) takes its
inspiration from the area's
traditional warehouses,
characterised by their wooden
post-and-beam construction
and brick façades.

The extensive glazing and roof lights, together with a rear façade entirely clad in translucent panels, make for a light-filled interior.

As befits a building dedicated to cycling, it is highly sustainable, using passive solar heating and natural ventilation while generating its own electricity via a series of rooftop solar panels.

BICYCLE FLAT
AMSTERDAM, THE NETHERLANDS 2001
VMX ARCHITECTS

The Bicycle Flat transports the thousands of bicycles usually found in front of the Centraal Station and houses them in a four-storey structure which owes more to a multi-storey car park than a bike shed.

By using the drop in height along the quay to their advantage, the architects were able to create a structure that rises from two storeys at its eastern end to four storeys in the west.

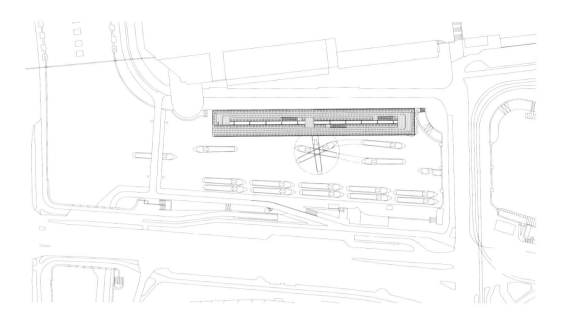

With space at a premium on
the narrow 100-metre long
site, the bike park is built
out over the water.

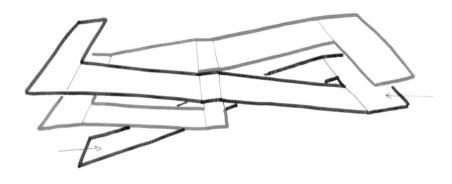

The sloping floors zig-zag
the length of the structure,
creating an exhilarating
series of switchbacks for
cyclists to negotiate.

The bike park's floors
are finished in the same
red asphalt used for the
country's cycle tracks.

ADMIRANT ENTRANCE BUILDING
EINDHOVEN, THE NETHERLANDS 2010
MASSIMILIANO AND DORIANA FUKSAS ARCHITECTS

A key element in the brief
to redevelop Eindhoven's
18 Septemberplein, one of the
city's major squares, was to
provide parking for 2,000
bicycles. The city wanted
to remove bikes from the
square to enable people to
move about freely, but still
wanted to encourage cycling.

By placing the bike park underground, the architects were able to create a shopper-friendly square. Cyclists enter the underground bike park via two cone-shaped enclosures that echo the form of the Admirant Entrance Building. Bicycles and riders are transported via travelators.

The Admirant Entrance Building forms a boundary to the square, its dynamic crystalline form providing a suitably grand entrance as well as a welcome distraction for the many cyclists who ride past each day.

A cyclist dismounts to make the short journey from bike path to the entrance of the bike park at the edge of 18 Septemberplein. The Admirant Entrance Building is on the right.

NØRREPORT TRAIN STATION
COPENHAGEN, DENMARK, CONSTRUCTION STARTED 2012
COBE AND GOTTLIEB PALUDAN ARCHITECTS

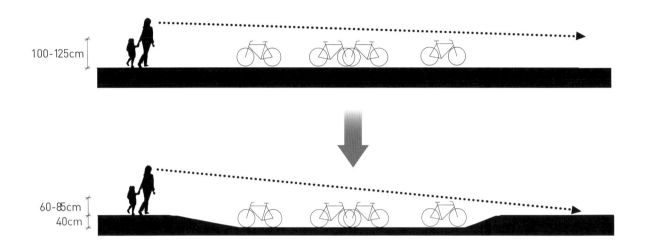

100-125cm

60-85cm
40cm

Described by the architects as "small pockets where you can peacefully park your bike before moving on", the beds are recessed 40 cm into the plaza and provide parking for up to 2,500 bicycles.

The redevelopment of Nørreport train station - the busiest in Denmark - takes the form of a large outdoor plaza punctuated by a series of circular pavilions. Topped by large, irregularly shaped overhanging roofs, these house the station's various functions. The bike beds are interspersed among the pavilions placing the bicycle at the heart of the scheme.

The bike beds are illuminated
at night by thousands of LEDs
that create islands of light
across the plaza.

BANKSIDE BIKESHED
LONDON, UK 2012
STUDIO MEDA

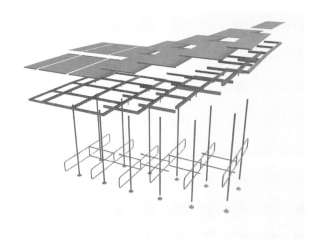

Studio Meda's competition-winning entry in the Bankside BikeShed competition has an economy of materials and simplicity of design that mean it can be constructed anywhere. Using a kit-of-parts approach, the BikeShed comprises a series of slim pillars topped by a flat overhanging roof. Horizontal bars attached to the pillars give extra stability for bikes, while lockers can be attached if required.

A prototype of the BikeShed was installed on London's Southbank in 2012 and has since been put into commercial production by Marshalls Street Furniture.

The elegance and restraint of
the Bankside BikeShed belie
its robust construction and
entirely utilitarian purpose.

BERMONDSEY BIKE STORE
LONDON, UK 2009
SARAH WIGGLESWORTH ARCHITECTS

Sarah Wigglesworth
Architects' Bermondsey
Bike Store has become a
centrepiece for a once
run-down area of southeast
London.

The bike store's façade, made
up from triangular steel
panels, is hung from a series
of 13 portal frames made from
Douglas fir. The translucent
GRP panels used for the
internal walls bathe the
interior in natural diffused
light.

The bicycle store resembles
- especially when lit up
at night - a jewelled box,
enhancing the square and
adding a welcome dash of
drama against the backdrop
of its more soberly suited
neighbours.

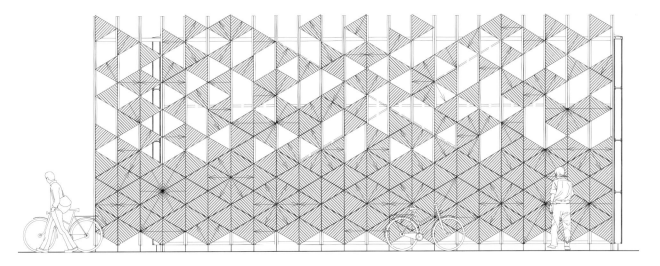

The practice has also designed a sustainable Christmas tree for the square which is made up of 35 recycled bike wheels and which can be used year after year.

There's space for 76 bicycles inside, all of which are reserved for residents and for those who work at the square.

NYC HOOP RACK AND NYC WRAP RACK
NEW YORK, USA 2008 ONWARDS
IAN MAHAFFY AND MAARTEN DE GREEVE

Ian Mahaffy and Maarten de Greeve won a 2008 competition organised by the New York City Department of Transport (DOT) to design a new standard bike rack for the city. Their elegant solution is now being rolled out across New York, with 5,000 racks in place at the time of writing.

Following on from the success of the NYC Hoop Rack, Mahaffy and de Greeve were commissioned by DOT to come up with a design to transform the city's unused parking-meter posts into bicycle stands as part of the city's ongoing programme to promote cycling. As of 2013, 12,000 racks had been installed.

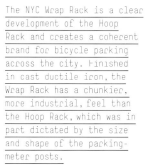

The NYC Wrap Rack is a clear development of the Hoop Rack and creates a coherent brand for bicycle parking across the city. Finished in cast ductile iron, the Wrap Rack has a chunkier, more industrial, feel than the Hoop Rack, which was in part dictated by the size and shape of the parking-meter posts.

Taking the form of an oversized bicycle wheel braced by a horizontal cross bar, the NYC Hoop Rack's simple yet robust form fits seamlessly into New York's many and varied districts.

THE BIKE HANGAR
VARIOUS LOCATIONS 2011
MANIFESTO ARCHITECTURE

As this New York mock-up demonstrates, the Bike Hangar has been designed for dense urban areas and is capable of slotting into the spaces between spaces. Its small footprint ensures that valuable floor space remains free for pedestrians.

Two Models

Multiple units of the standing version can be connected in a series to infinitely increase its storage capacity.

Solar Panel
Advertisement Space
Card Reader

BH-6

Parking Capacity: 6
Dimension:
H: 7,570mm (24'-10")
D: 1,730mm (5'-8")
W: 6,800mm (22'-4")

BH-15

Parking Capacity: 15
Dimension:
H: 15,570mm (51'-1")
D: 1,730mm (5'-8")
W: 6,800mm (22'-4")

Multiple Unit Installation

The Bike Hangar is capable of storing up to 15 bikes vertically by means of a belt-driven carousel. The system can be extended laterally, if space allows, creating multiple hangar systems.

The Bike Hangar is essentially a giant chain-and-sprocket set driven by pedalling a modified bike attached to its base. Users rotate the carousel until a free hangar is available, attach their bike and then leave (or vice versa). Access is via a digital-card reader powered by integrated solar panels set in the carousel's roof.

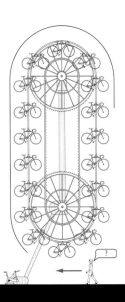  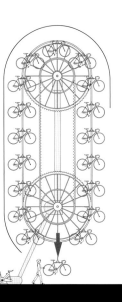 

A prototype of the six-bike
version was installed at the
Gwangju Design Biennale in
Korea in 2011.

115

BICYCLE TRANSIT CENTRE
WASHINGTON DC, USA 2011
KGP DESIGN STUDIO

AXIAL LOADING DIAGRAM

┄┄┄┄> tension force
<────> compression force

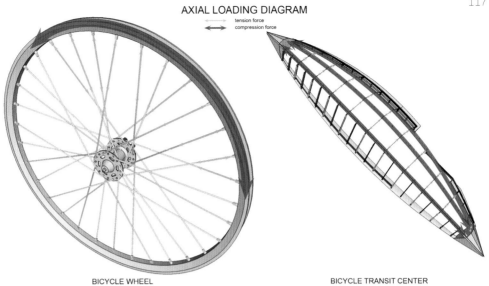

BICYCLE WHEEL   BICYCLE TRANSIT CENTER

The Bicycle Transit Center's form echoes the shape of a bicycle helmet, while its structural logic is influenced by the bicycle wheel. A series of arched steel tubes - held in compression at either end by a pair of concrete wedges - span the structure much like the rim of a wheel. These are in turn stabilised by steel tie rods that act like spokes.

The centre has parking for 150 bicycles, as well as changing facilities, lockers, and a workshop.

The structure is entirely clad in glass: on the western elevation, this consists of a single plane articulated by a series of vertical louvres and a surface frit to provide solar protection, while on the eastern side the glass is stepped up in a series of interlocking planes.

By placing such an uncompromisingly modern building next to the Beaux-Arts splendour of Union Station, its designers are asking us to consider the bicycle on equal terms with the train as an alternative mode of transport for the twenty-first century.

CYCLING ARENAS
AND BICYCLE DISPLAYS

CYCLING ARENAS
AND BICYCLE DISPLAYS

Architects have long celebrated the speed and dynamism of the bicycle through the velodrome. Though velodromes were first developed in the mid-nineteenth century, it wasn't until 1895 - ten years after the introduction of the Safety Bicycle - that the standard oval shape we know today began to dominate. Like the bicycle, velodromes have retained much the same format ever since. However, despite these constraints some of the world's greatest architects have been drawn to the velodrome and in the process have designed some remarkable structures, not least those stadia completed for various Olympic Games, including Santiago Calatrava's Athens velodrome and Dominique Perrault's Berlin track from 1997, created for the city's ultimately unsuccessful bid for the 2000 games.

The latest, designed by Hopkins Architects for the London 2012 Olympic Games, is not only the fastest in the world but also the most sustainable. The team responsible wanted to create a building that replicated the inherent efficiency of the bicycle's design. The result is a lightweight, highly sustainable building whose iconic roof reflects the geometry of the track it encloses. The roof's double curving cable-net structure ensures that its weight is less than half that of the velodrome completed for the Beijing Olympics. The relationship between the track - made from sustainably sourced Siberian pine - and the exterior is emphasised by the use of timber cladding. Nicknamed the 'Pringle' by the British public, its iconic status was assured by Team GB's stellar performance on the track.

BIG architects created an alternative kind of bicycle arena for Shanghai Expo 2010. Designed to distil the essence of Denmark in the heart of China, the building put the bicycle at its centre. The bike is a national symbol in both China and Denmark, although in China it is becoming usurped by the motor car as an expanding middle class abandon it in favour of the internal combustion engine. Denmark on the other hand, as is amply illustrated throughout this book, has some of the most cycle-friendly policies and infrastructure in the world. BIG's pavilion celebrates this by enabling visitors to jump on one of Copenhagen's city bikes and explore the building and its exhibits from the bicycle seat. The looping paths - painted in Denmark's signature blue - take visitors in and out of the building from the pool at the bottom, which provided a temporary home to Copenhagen's Little Mermaid, to the rooftop viewing deck and bike park.

Zaha Hadid's transport museum on the banks of the River Clyde in Glasgow houses an altogether different kind of velodrome. Designed by Event Communications, the museum's Hanging Bicycle Velodrome is formed from a suspended Mobius strip. Made up of 360 pairs of steel fins, each of which is fixed to a 13.5-metre tubular-steel ring, the velodrome carries 31 bicycles drawn from the Museum's permanent collection. Highlights include a number of classic Scottish road bikes such as the Baxter Special and Flying Scot and the revolutionary carbon Lotus Sport Monocoque that smashed a number of track and time-trial records.

> Architect Michael Embacher's bicycle collection is no less impressive. Since beginning in earnest in 2003, he has amassed more than 200 bicycles, all of which are rare, unusual, or even flawed. The bicycles are regularly displayed around the world in exhibitions designed by the architect himself. The guiding design principle behind all of these shows is the desire to convey the dynamism and lightness of the bicycle, and to impress upon visitors that this is an object built for speed and movement. Embacher achieves this by suspending the bicycles from the ceiling so that they can be viewed at eye level. Each is then arranged along curved routes, allowing visitors to walk among them and imagine what it is like to corner at speed.

In contrast, the Parkcycle Swarm is a mobile, human-powered exhibition space that can transform urban areas into instant public parks. Designed by Copenhagen-based N55 in conjunction with Till Wolfer and John Bela, the Parkcycle Swarm is based on the XYZ Cargo Cycle and has been developed to reclaim those areas normally used by cars such as car parks or roads. Consisting of a lightweight aluminium space-frame which is then covered in faux turf and fitted over the cargo bike the Swarm can be ridden anywhere to form an urban oasis. Democratic in nature, the designers view the Parkcycle Swarm as a DIY urban planning tool and hope others will build their own cycles and influence their neighbourhoods as an alternative to the top-down urban planning which dominates most cities.

LONDON VELODROME
LONDON, UK 2012
HOPKINS ARCHITECTS

Nicknamed the Pringle by the British public because of its distinctive double-curving roof, its iconic status was assured after Team GB won seven gold medals on the track in the London 2012 Olympics.

Made from sustainably sourced
Siberian pine, the track was
designed by Ron Webb, who was
also responsible for the
tracks used in the Sydney and
Athens Olympics.

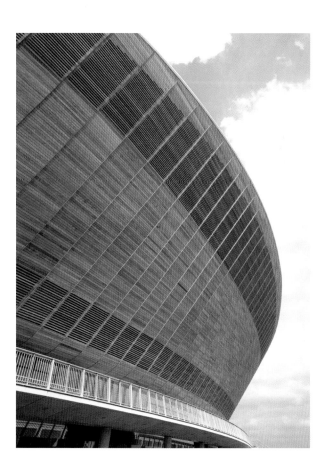

The upper bowl of the
velodrome, which is clad in
red cedar wood, appears to
float above the fully glazed
concourse level.

BICYCLE CLUB
SANYA, CHINA 2012 (WORK BEGAN)
NL ARCHITECTS

The roof appears to float
above the glass pavilion
below, its large overhangs
providing welcome shade
from the tropical climate.

The velodrome's angles have
been kept deliberately low,
ranging from 12 degrees to a
maximum of 33 degrees - some
way short of a full-size
track. A turning zone has
also been incorporated at the
top of the stairs so that
less-confident cyclists need
not complete a full lap.

Located in the Chinese
holiday resort of Sanya, the
Bicycle Club combines bike
hire and sales facilities
with a mini rooftop
velodrome. However, at just
100 metres, the Bicycle
Club's rooftop track is
designed primarily for those
wanting to test-ride bicycles
from the shop below rather
than out-and-out racers.

DANISH PAVILION SHANGHAI EXPO
SHANGHAI, CHINA 2010
BIG ARCHITECTS

Footpaths have been provided
for those visitors wishing
to take a more leisurely
approach to the exhibits.
As in any Danish city,
pedestrians coexist happily
alongside cyclists.

In order to give visitors to
the Danish pavilion a real
taste of Copenhagen, BIG
placed the bicycle at the
centre of the scheme. Over
300 city bikes were
provided, while the bike
paths were finished in the
traditional blue of Denmark's
cycle infrastructure to
ensure visitors received
the full experience.

The pavilion was designed around a double loop that takes cyclists in and out of the building, enabling them to experience the various exhibits directly from the bicycle saddle.

The pavilion's façade,
constructed from white-
painted steel to help keep
it cool, was perforated
in a pattern that reflects
the structural stresses
it experiences.

OMNISPORTSCENTRUM
APELDOORN, THE NETHERLANDS 2008
FAULKNERBROWNS ARCHITECTS

As the Dutch national centre
for indoor athletics, cycling
and volleyball, the venue
regularly hosts international
events, not least the
UCI Track Cycling World
Championships in March 2011.
The geometry of both the
cycle and athletics tracks
has been carefully integrated
to enable sections to be
removed, thus opening up
the infield for a variety
of other sporting and
entertainment events.

The Omnisportscentrum,
designed with flexibility
in mind, incorporates both
a 250-metre cycle track
and a 200-metre athletics
track. Further facilities
include a multifunctional
sports hall, outdoor skating
rink, football pitches,
and accommodation.

GLASGOW RIVERSIDE TRANSPORT MUSEUM, UK 2011

ZAHA HADID ARCHITECTS

The bicycles come from the museum's permanent collection and include a number of classic Scottish bikes such as the Baxter Special and Flying Scot, as well as a Lotus Sport Monocoque, similar to that used by Chris Boardman when he broke the 4,000-metre pursuit record at the Barcelona Olympics.

The museum's sinuous zinc-clad roof draws on the city's industrial heritage, evoking images of shipbuilding and providing a reference point for what is displayed inside.

Looking south to the River Clyde, the vast, column-free interior space is flooded with light.

Overleaf: Designed by Event Communications, the museum's innovative Hanging Bicycle Velodrome is formed from a suspended Mobius strip. Thirty-one bicycles are arranged along its continuous surface, which is made up of 360 pairs of steel fins, each of which is fixed to a 13.5-metre tubular-steel ring.

DERBY MULTI-SPORTS ARENA
DERBY, UK 2013 (CONSTRUCTION BEGAN)
FAULKNERBROWNS ARCHITECTS

While the focal point of the Derby Multi-Sport Arena is its raised cycle track, its infield will also accommodate badminton, basketball, netball and volleyball.

Britain has dominated the sport of track cycling in recent years, and facilities such as the Derby Velodrome, the UK's fifth 250-metre track, which is scheduled to open in 2014, can only enhance this success.

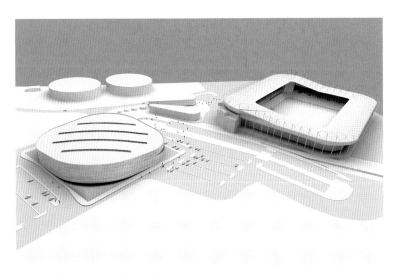

As well as having an international-standard velodrome, the area surrounding the arena will contain an outdoor 1.5-km closed-road circuit.

The bicycles are regularly
displayed around the world
in exhibitions designed by
Embacher. The exhibition at
the MAK in Vienna in 2013
employed the same suspended
metal hanging-system as
Portland, enabling visitors
to view the bikes at
eye-level.

Among the curios from the Embacher collection on display at the Portland Art Museum in 2013 was a KIRK Precision road bike (pp.148-149). Now extremely rare, the bike was made from highly flammable magnesium, which resulted in the factory burning down just a few days into its production. Equally eccentric is the Skoot (below), which when not in use can be transformed into a suitcase.

Architect Michael Embacher's collection includes more than 200 bicycles, all of which are rare, unusual, or even flawed. As can be seen from these bicycles on show in Portland, the collection covers everything from cargo bikes to racers.

The exhibits - seen here in Vienna - are arranged along curved routes to help convey the inherent dynamism and lightness of the bicycle.

OLYMPIC VELODROME
ATHENS, GREECE 2004
SANTIAGO CALATRAVA

The stadium has a 5,500-seat
capacity, and its 250-metre
long, 7.5-metre wide Afzelia-
wood track is one of the
fastest in the world.

Originally built in 1991 for
the Mediterranean Games, the
Olympic Velodrome underwent
an extensive refurbishment
for the 2004 Athens Olympics.
While the Velodrome was
previously entirely open,
Calatrava covered it with
a soaring roof suspended from
a pair of massive tubular-
steel arches.

A delicate cat's cradle
suspends the glass-and-steel
roof from the two 45-metre
high arches, allowing it to
hover above the track and
leaving the sides exposed to
the elements.

Calatrava not only redesigned the velodrome and Olympic Stadium - which employs a similar roof structure to the cycle track - but also master-planned the entire park, designing everything from the hard and soft landscaping to the series of grand entrance gates and covered walkways which help to unify the vast site.

OLYMPIC VELODROME
BERLIN, GERMANY 1997
DOMINIQUE PERRAULT ARCHITECTURE

At 142 metres in diameter, the velodrome's steel roof is the largest of its kind in Europe. Like the Olympic swimming pool, it's covered in a fine wire gauze which shimmers in the sunlight.

Sunk into their central Berlin site, both buildings are surrounded by an orchard of apple trees. The architect's intention was that the buildings would appear as two 'tables' - one round, one rectangular - among the green landscaping.

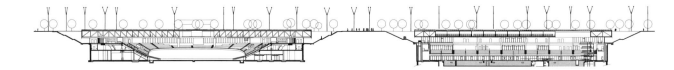

Dominique Perrault
Architecture won an
international competition to
design the Berlin Velodrome
and Olympic swimming pool in
1992 in support of the city's
ultimately unsuccessful bid
to host the 2000 Olympics.

The magnificent space-frame
roof resembles a huge spoked
wheel. The 250-metre track is
made from Siberian spruce.

PARKCYCLE SWARM
COPENHAGEN, DENMARK 2013
N55 WITH TILL WOLFER
AND JOHN BELA FROM REBAR GROUP

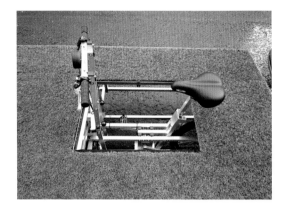

A lightweight aluminium space-frame is fitted over the cargo bike and covered with faux turf to create the park. An openable flap enables the 'garden' to be cycled to its destination.

The Parkcycle Swarm is a human-powered mobile garden which can be deployed to create an instant public park. It is designed to reclaim areas normally used by cars, such as car parks or roads, in order to encourage peaceful, non-polluting social activities.

Based on N55's XYZ Cargo
Cycle, the Parkcycle Swarm is
a collaboration between N55,
Till Wolfer and John Bela
from the Rebar group.

Viewing the Parkcycle Swarm
as a DIY urban-planning tool,
the designers hope it will
not only inspire others to
build their own cycles, but
also encourage them, as an
alternative to the top-
down urban planning which
dominates most cities, to
have a direct influence on
their neighbourhoods.

ACKNOWLEDGEMENTS

This book is very much a collaborative effort. I am indebted to my editor Curt Holtz at Prestel who helped to refine and redefine the original concept, and to his colleagues Stella Sämann and Dorothea Bethke for taking it forward; to designer Joana Niemeyer for bringing it to life, and to the many architects and designers whose projects feature and whose insights and enthusiasm made it such a pleasure to work on. I would also like to thank all those photographers who contributed images and without whom this book would not have been possible. I am particularly grateful to Seamus Masters, who is not only a talented photographer but also a fellow cycling enthusiast and regular riding companion. For my wife Liz and son Hector.

Gavin Blyth is a London-based writer and editor specialising in architecture and design. He has contributed to several books on the subject, including *Norman Foster: Works 6* (Prestel) and *Dymaxion Car: Buckminster Fuller* (Ivorypress). When not writing and thinking about architecture, he can usually be found cycling in London or the Kent countryside.

PICTURE
CREDITS

Front cover: Santiago Calatrava, Peace Bridge, Calgary,
Canada, photograph © Joshua Dool, Vancover
Back cover: © Seamus Masters

Prestel Verlag, Munich
A member of Verlagsgruppe Random House GmbH

Prestel Verlag
Neumarkter Strasse 28
81673 Munich
Tel. +49 (0)89 4136-0
Fax   +49 (0)89 4136-2335

Prestel Publishing Ltd.
14-17 Wells Street
London W1T 3PD
Tel. +44 (0)20 7323-5004
Fax   +44 (0)20 7323-0271

Prestel Publishing
900 Broadway, Suite 603
New York, NY 10003
Tel. +1 (212) 995-2720
Fax   +1 (212) 995-2733

www.prestel.com

Library of Congress Control Number: 2014933443; British
Library Cataloguing-in-Publication Data: a catalogue record
for this book is available from the British Library;
Deutsche Nationalbibliothek holds a record of this
publication in the Deutsche Nationalbibliografie; detailed
bibliographical data can be found under: www.dnb.de

Prestel books are available worldwide. Please contact
your nearest bookseller or one of the above addresses for
information concerning your local distributor.

Editorial direction: Stella Sämann, Dorothea Bethke
Copyediting: Chris Murray
Design and layout: Joana Niemeyer, April, London
Production: Astrid Wedemeyer
Origination: Reproline Mediateam, Munich
Printing and binding: DZS Grafik, Ljubljana

Verlagsgruppe Random House FSC®N001967
The FSC®-certified paper Condat Matt Perigord is
produced by mill Condat, Le Lardin Saint-Lazare, France.

Printed in Slovenia

ISBN 978-3-7913-4909-1